Planes Have Wings

and other questions
about transportation

Christopher Maynard

KINGFISHER
NEW YORK

KINGFISHER
LONDON & NEW YORK

Copyright © Kingfisher 2012
Published in the United States by Kingfisher,
175 Fifth Ave., New York, NY 10010
Kingfisher is an imprint of Macmillan Children's Books,
London.
All rights reserved.

First published 1993 by Kingfisher
This edition published 2012 by Kingfisher

Consultant: Ian Graham

Distributed in the U.S. and Canada by Macmillan,
175 Fifth Ave., New York, NY 10010

Library of Congress Cataloging-in-Publication data
has been applied for.

ISBN 978-0-7534-6704-6 (HC)
ISBN 978-0-7534-6703-9 (PB)

Kingfisher books are available for special promotions and
premiums. For details contact: Special Markets Department,
Macmillan, 175 Fifth Ave., New York, NY 10010.

For more information, please visit www.kingfisherbooks.com

Printed in China
9 8 7 6 5 4 3 2 1
1TR/1011/WKT/UG/140MA

Illustrations: Mark Bergin cover, 5 (train, car, and bike), 8,
11t, 16, 20–21, 30–31 (aircraft); Chris Forsey 4, 5 (plane), 6–7,
17–19, 26 (wagon train), 28–29; Tony Kenyon (B. L. Kearley
Ltd.) all cartoons; Sebastian Quigley (Linden Artists) 10, 11b;
Ian Thompson 9, 12–13; Ross Watton (Garden Studio) 14–15,
22–25, 30 (transporter), 31 (ships).

CONTENTS

4 How far can I go in an hour?

6 Which is the fastest car?

6 Which is the fastest boat?

7 Which is the fastest plane?

8 Why do planes have wings?

8 Which cars have wings?

10 Which plane is the biggest?

11 Can planes hover in the air?

12 Do airships run on air?

13 Why do hot-air balloons float?

14 Why do cars have wheels?

15 Which are the biggest tires?

15 Which boats have wheels?

16 Why do cars need gas?

17 What happens inside car engines?

18 Who cycled over the sea?

18 Can bikes climb mountains?

19 How many people can ride on a bike?

20 Can motorcycles ever fly?

21 Which motorcycles have four wheels?

21 What is the largest human motorcycle pyramid?

22 Why don't ships sink?

22 How do submarines sink?

23 Which ships fly?

24 Which are the biggest ships?

24 What were longships?

25 Which are the world's smallest boats?

26 Why don't trains fall off the rails?

27 What were wagon trains?

28 Do road trains run on rails?

29 Can trains float?

30 Which plane hitches a ride?

31 When do cars hitch rides?

32 Index

How far can I go in an hour?

If you keep walking for an hour and don't stop to take any rests, your own two legs will carry you about 2.5 miles (4km). You will be able to go farther if you run, but you will probably have to keep stopping to catch your breath. The easiest way to travel more than a few miles is to get something to carry you!

It would take an ordinary garden snail more than three days to get as far as you can walk in one hour.

Trotting on a pony for an hour, you would be able to travel three times as far as you would on foot.

To walk as far as a jumbo jet can carry you in an hour, you would have to keep going for ten days and nights!

Racing cyclists can pedal at least ten times as fast as you can walk. They can cover as much as 25 miles (40km) in an hour.

Aircraft are the fastest way to travel. Flying high up above the clouds in a jumbo jet, you would be able to get from Los Angeles, California, to New York City in less than five hours.

Riding a high-speed train like the Japanese bullet train or the French TGV, you can travel at least twice as fast as you can in a car.

Engines are more powerful than muscles, so machines can carry you much faster than legs. Riding in a car on a highway, you can travel at more than 60 miles per hour (100km/h)!

Even if you stay in bed all day, you will travel about 1.5 million miles (2.5 million km)! That's how far Earth moves through space in 24 hours as it goes around the Sun.

Which is the fastest car?

A British car named *Thrust 2* set the world land-speed record in 1983. A new record was then set in 1997 by *Thrust SSC*, which reached a speed of 763 miles per hour (1,228km/h).

The first car to go faster than 60 miles per hour (100km/h) was battery powered. It was named *La Jamais Contente*, and it did this more than 100 years ago, in 1899.

The world's fastest sailing craft are sailboards. In good winds, they can zip across the water at more than 50 miles per hour (80km/h).

Which is the fastest boat?

Hydroplanes skim over the water almost as if flying. In 1978, Ken Warby roared to 318 miles per hour (511km/h) in his jet-powered *Spirit of Australia*.

Spirit of Australia

Thrust 2

To carry astronauts to the Moon in the 1960s and 1970s, the Saturn V rockets had to travel more than 40 times as fast as a jumbo jet. But the top speed of the astronauts' Moon buggy was only 8 miles per hour (13 km/h)!

turbo by Faberge

NGKN

SR-71A "Blackbird"

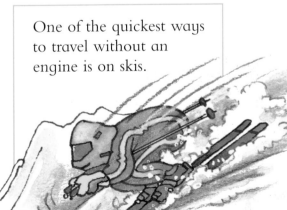

One of the quickest ways to travel without an engine is on skis.

Which is the fastest plane?

The fastest aircraft are planes with jet engines. The world record was set back in 1976, when the United States' SR-71A reached an amazing 2,193 miles per hour (3,530 km/h)! It was nicknamed "Blackbird."

Why do planes have wings?

Planes have wings for the same reason that birds do—to help them fly. Plane wings work because of their shape. They are curved more on top than underneath, and this makes air flow faster above them than below. The faster air above the wings sucks them upward.

Which cars have wings?

Wing

Many racecars have wings—upside-down ones, curved more underneath than on top. This means that they work in the opposite way to plane wings, sucking down rather than up, helping the tires grip the track.

We can't flap our arms fast enough to fly like birds. But this didn't keep people from trying to copy birds in the days before planes were invented!

Rotor blade

A helicopter's long, thin rotor blades are wing shaped—curved more on top than underneath. As they whirl through the air, this wing shape helps the helicopter fly.

Hydroplane

To see how wings work, blow hard over the top of a piece of thin paper. The paper will rise up!

Submarines have short wings called hydroplanes. These are moved up and down to help subs climb and dive.

9

Which plane is the biggest?

The biggest passenger plane is the A380 airliner. It carries about 525 passengers. They sit on two decks, one above the other. The biggest plane of all is a giant cargo plane called the An-225. Only one was built. It can carry cargo weighing as much as 25 elephants inside its huge body.

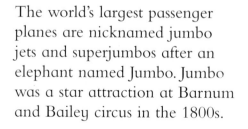

The world's largest passenger planes are nicknamed jumbo jets and superjumbos after an elephant named Jumbo. Jumbo was a star attraction at Barnum and Bailey circus in the 1800s.

Can planes hover in the air?

Most planes have to keep going fast through the air to fly. If they slow down and stop, their wings stop working and they can't fly anymore. The F-35B Lightning II (above) and the Harrier (below) can hover in one spot above the ground by blasting jets of air straight downward to hold them up.

Hummingbirds can hover in the air, too. They beat their tiny wings between eight and 80 times per second. They can also fly backward and upside down!

Harrier fighter planes have been nicknamed "jump jets" because they can take off straight up into the air.

Do airships run on air?

Modern airships should really be called gas ships, because they use a gas called helium to help them fly. Helium helps airships float because it is lighter than air.

The bag of an airship is called an envelope.

Fairground balloons are usually filled with helium gas. To see which is lighter, helium or air, try letting go of a fairground balloon at the same time as a party balloon filled with air.

The first "air" letter was carried by a balloon.

Why do hot-air balloons float?

Balloons float because hot air rises, and hot air rises because it is lighter than cold air. The air inside a hot-air balloon is heated by a burner that works like a camping gas stove.

Burner

The first-ever balloon passengers were a rooster, a duck, and a sheep! Their eight-minute flight took place over Paris, France, in 1783.

13

Why do cars have wheels?

 Cars and most other land machines have wheels because they make them easier to move. Things slow down when they rub against the ground. Wheels help because they turn easily, and only a small part of them touches the ground.

Imagine how difficult it would be to move a car if all of it was touching the ground, instead of just its wheels!

The world's longest car has 26 wheels. It even has room for a tiny swimming pool onboard!

Snow and ice are much more slippery than soil and rocks. That's why skis and ice skates don't need wheels.

14

Which are the biggest tires?

The world's biggest tires are made for huge dump trucks to cushion their heavy loads of rocks and earth. The tires are more than 13 feet (4m) high—that's about four times as tall as you are!

The wheelbarrow was invented in China more than 1,800 years ago. It made it easier to carry heavy loads.

Which boats have wheels?

Riverboats called paddleboats are driven along by wheels. The wheels have wide boards called paddles. As the wheels turn, the paddles push against the water, moving the boats along.

Why do cars need gas?

Many toy cars use electrical energy, stored in batteries. There are ordinary cars that run on batteries, too.

A car needs gasoline for the same reason that you need food—to give it energy to move. It's hard to tell by looking at it, but gas has lots of energy locked up inside it. This energy is set free inside a car engine so that it can be used to turn road wheels.

Gasoline is made from oil, and it has energy because it comes from things that were once living! Oil was formed millions of years ago, from the bodies of tiny plants and animals.

Piston

Each piston moves up and down inside a cylinder.

16

Gas is kept in a tank. It is pumped along a pipe to the engine.

Gas tank

What happens inside car engines?

Gasoline is mixed with air inside a car engine and then set on fire by an electric spark. This makes the air and gas explode with a bang. This explosion pushes engine parts called pistons up and down very quickly. The pistons make a rod called the crankshaft spin around. The crankshaft makes other rods spin, and they turn the car's wheels.

Spark plug

Spark

Piston

Cylinder

Crankshaft

Who cycled over the sea?

In June 1979, American Bryan Allen pedaled a special plane called *Gossamer Albatross* across the English Channel, from England to France, in just under two hours and 50 minutes. Nine years later, Kanellos Kanellopoulos of Greece pedaled his *Daedalus 88* over the sea between the islands of Crete and Santorini.

Can bikes climb mountains?

Machines called mountain bikes are specially designed for rough, stony ground. Their frames are extra strong so that they can stand up to rattling over bumps, while their knobby tires grip well even in slippery sand or mud.

It's not easy to balance on a unicycle—it has only one wheel!

How many people can ride on a bike?

When the first bicycles were invented about 200 years ago, they didn't have any pedals! People rolled them along by pushing against the ground with their feet.

Although most bikes are designed for one rider, special bikes are sometimes built to take more. A bike was built in Belgium that had seats and pedals for 35 people, but it was very difficult for them all to balance and ride at the same time!

Can motorcycles ever fly?

Motorcycles can't really fly because they don't have wings, but stunt riders still do amazing things on them. By speeding up a ramp and taking off from the end, riders can make their machines leap huge distances through the air.

The first motorcycle with a gasoline engine was built in 1885. Much of the bike was carved from wood! It was destroyed by a fire in 1903.

Which motorcycles have four wheels?

Quad bikes are special cross-country motorcycles with four wheels to grip and balance on rough ground.

Quad bikes are also called all-terrain vehicles. *Terrain* means "land" or "ground."

Some motorcycles are called choppers because they have had parts "chopped off" and moved around to make them look unusual.

What is the largest human motorcycle pyramid?

For more than two people to ride one motorcycle is difficult and dangerous, but there are stunt riders who do it for special shows. In 2001, the Dare Devils team of the Indian Army Signal Corps managed to carry 201 people on a line of ten motorcycles at a military parade ground in Jabalpur.

Why don't ships sink?

When things are put into water, they make room for themselves by pushing the water aside. Although ships are heavy, they are hollow with high sides. This means that they can settle quite low in the water, pushing a lot of the water aside. In fact, a ship will not sink unless it is overloaded and becomes heavier than the water it pushes aside.

You push water aside when you get into a bathtub. That's why you have to be careful not to overfill it!

How do submarines sink?

Submarines sink by making themselves too heavy to float. Water is let into special tanks to add weight. When it's time for a submarine to resurface, the water is pushed out.

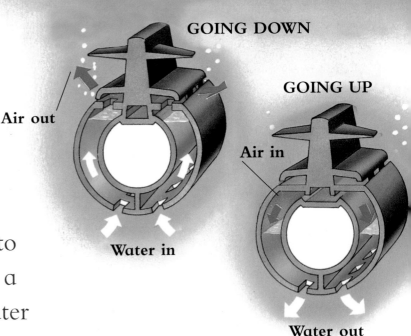

GOING DOWN

GOING UP

Air out

Air in

Water in

Water out

Which ships fly?

Although hovercraft travel across water, they don't float on it like ships. Instead, they hover just above the waves, held up by a cushion of air.

Hovercraft can travel over land as well as water.

Tanker

This strange-looking diving suit was invented more than 200 years ago. The tubes carried air to and from the surface.

One of the earliest submarines was built by Dutchman Cornelius van Drebbel and tested in the 1620s. Twelve oarsmen rowed a wooden boat below the surface of the River Thames in England.

Which are the biggest ships?

The biggest ships in the world are oil supertankers. They can be more than 0.3 mile (0.5km) long and weigh more than 1,000 jumbo jets. Giant tankers can take 20 minutes to stop!

Life jackets are only 200 years old. A French priest invented them when he lined a waistcoat with a floaty material called cork.

Some tankers are so long that crews cycle on them!

Tanker

What were longships?

We call Viking ships longships, because of their long, thin shape. The Vikings were people who lived in Scandinavia about 1,000 years ago. They built sturdy wooden ships and were skilled sailors.

Viking ships could be rowed or sailed. They had a single square sail.

24

Which are the world's smallest boats?

Coracles are just about the world's smallest boats—they usually have room for only one person!

Sailboat

Hovercraft

Viking ship

Warships once had small castles at the front and back.

Sterncastle

Forecastle

Ships' hammocks were first used 500 years ago. European sailors copied them from hanging beds they saw in the West Indies.

Why don't trains fall off the rails?

Trains have metal wheels and run on narrow metal rails. Metal can be very slippery, so train wheels are specially shaped to keep them from falling off. The inside of each wheel has a lip called a flange that holds it on the rail.

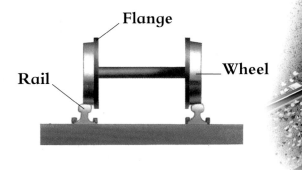

Flange

Rail

Wheel

The wagons rolled along at 1–2 miles per hour (1.5–3km/h).

Some trains can climb steep mountainsides without sliding down. They have an extra wheel with a toothed edge that "bites" into a notched rail.

Early American locomotives were fitted with plowlike cowcatchers to keep the line ahead clear.

What were wagon trains?

In the 1800s, when settlers spread westward across North America, they took all of their belongings with them in huge wagons pulled by oxen or mules. Families traveled in groups. Their wagons following one another in a long line were called a wagon train.

Do road trains run on rails?

No, road trains run on roads. They are called trains because they are made up of trucks pulling many trailers, in the same way that locomotives pull cars.

Not all trains need drivers. Some city trains are controlled by computers.

Australian trucks and cars often have strong metal bull bars attached in front to cut down damage if they hit large animals, such as kangaroos or cattle, on outback roads. Another name for them is roo bars (*roo* is short for "kangaroo").

Streetcars are buses with metal wheels that run on rails. They use electricity to move, taking it from cables stretched high up above the road.

Bull bars

Road trains are often used in areas where there are no railroad lines—in parts of the Australian outback, for example.

Can trains float?

Maglevs are passenger trains that float just above a special track. They are lifted and driven by the power of magnets, and they can travel very fast—at more than 300 miles per hour (500km/h)!

Which plane hitches a ride?

It's not every day that you see one plane hitching a ride on another, but it does happen. A rocket plane called *SpaceShip Two* is designed to hitch a ride underneath an aircraft called *White Knight 2*. When they reach a height of about 50,000 feet (15,200m), *White Knight 2* drops *SpaceShip Two*, which fires its rocket engine and soars away into space at 2,500 miles per hour (4,000km/h).

Ships can ride piggyback, too, on special heavy-lift ships! First, the heavy-lift ship makes itself sink—not completely, but low enough for a smaller ship to float onto its deck. When it rises up again, the smaller ship gets a ride.

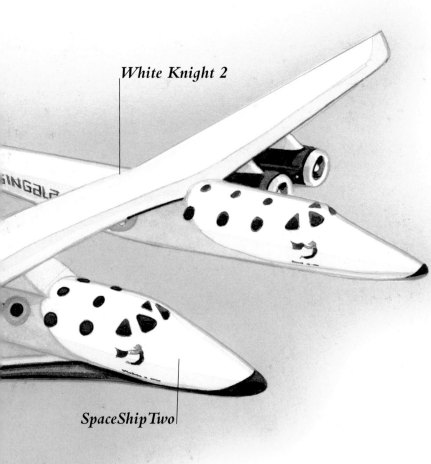

White Knight 2

SpaceShip Two

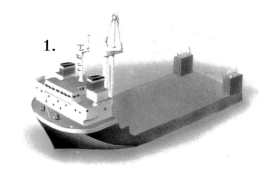

1.

2.

3.

When do cars hitch rides?

It's usually people that hitch rides in cars, but sometimes cars themselves get taken for a ride. It happens when new cars are carried on trucks or trains, from the factories where they are made to the show rooms where they are sold.

It may sometimes look as if cars are about to roll off transporters, but don't worry—they are tied firmly in place.

Index

A

aircraft 5, 7, 8, 9, 10–11, 18, 30
airships 12–13
all-terrain vehicles 21

B

balloons 12–13
bicycles 18–19
boats 6, 15, 25 *see also* ships
bullet trains 5

C

cars 5, 6, 8, 14, 16–17, 31
choppers (motorcycles) 21
coracles 25

D

dump trucks 15

E

engines 6, 7, 17

F

F-35B Lightning II 11
floating 22, 29
flying 8–9
fuel *see* gasoline

G

gasoline 16, 17

H

Harriers 11
helicopters 9
horse riding 4
hot-air balloons 12–13
hovercraft 23
hummingbirds 11
hydroplanes 6

J

jumbo jets 4, 5, 10
jump jets 11

L

locomotives 27
longships, Viking 24

M

maglevs 29
Moon buggies 7
motorcycles 20–21
mountain bikes 18

O

oil tankers 24

P

paddleboats 15
planes *see* aircraft

R

racecars 8
rails, train 26
road trains 28, 29

S

sailboards 6
ships 22–25, 31
   see also boats
skates 14
skis 7
space rockets 7
SpaceShip Two 30
streetcars 29
submarines 9, 22, 23

T

TGVs 5
tires 8, 15, 18
trains 5, 26–27, 29
transporters 30–31
trucks 28–29, 31

U

unicycles 19

W

wagon trains 26, 27
wheels 14–15, 19
White Knight 2 30
wings 8–9, 11